With One
Blink

With One Blink

A GUIDE

TO ENLIGHTENMENT

AND EMPOWERMENT

IN THE FACE OF

ADVERSITY

KELLEY DELLA VECCHIA

For information about this title or to order other books and/or electronic
media, contact the publisher:

Kelley Della Vecchia
kelleydellavecchia05@gmail.com

ISBN: 978-1-7360541-0-9 (softcover)
           978-1-7360541-1-6 (eBook)

Printed in the United States of America

Cover and Interior design: 1106 Design

Introduction

Writing ...

I remember hating it in grade school. The ideas never really flowed out as quickly as I had hoped. My mind always worked a lot faster than my hand could write. And now, I seem to rely on it daily—kinda like free therapy where I can be alone with my thoughts.

This book has been years in the making. Actually, I should have started it the first time I was diagnosed with cancer, but I dragged my feet for some reason. Maybe it was because I knew deep down that my story had only just begun, and I'd have so much more to tell.

So as you read through the pages of this book, please know that my heart went into writing it. If you are holding it in your hands at this moment, it's because you need something. Maybe you need some hope. Maybe you want some inspiration to get through a tough time. Or maybe the title speaks to you. Wherever you are in your life, I hope my words give you exactly what you need at this very moment.

Chapter One

What It Was *Supposed to Be*

Think back to when you were a little kid. Maybe you had a tough upbringing or maybe your early years were picture-perfect, but all of us, at some point, had instilled in us the notion of what our future is *"supposed to be."* (I'll come back to that notion a lot in this chapter.) You were taught life should look a certain way according to the beliefs and priorities of the people who raised you. Some dreamed of having the white picket fence and being a perfect spouse and perfect parent. Others strived for that CEO position to feel the rush of power. Nonetheless, you had what was *supposed to be* imprinted on your young mind.

I believe this is where disappointment and lack of fulfillment come from. When you're driven by the desires of other people, you exist to please everyone around you. But what about pleasing yourself?

My whole life, I was the good girl, the one who sang and danced and played sports. I had lots of friends, loved people, and enjoyed making them happy. I had a vivid imagination and painted the world rose-colored. I smiled often and wore my heart on my sleeve.

Why? I was trained that way. It's what I thought *I* was *supposed to be.*

Let me explain: From what I know, my biological father and my mom had a sweet beginning to their lives together. I remember my mom telling me the story of when she wanted to get engaged. Like all girls, she dreamed about the perfect stone and number of "carats" her ring would be. One day, my father got down on his knee. As my mom excitedly thought that THIS was her moment, he slowly opened a ring box with a real "carrot" stick inside.

He thought it was hilarious. My mom—not so much. It still makes me giggle to this day, because that sense of humor is something I gravitate toward when I meet people.

I look back now at pictures, and I think they resemble Elvis and Priscilla Presley in the way they looked and in how I've imagined their love story.

They were together a few years, and they divorced when I was about two. At first, it was a typical divorce custody schedule: My dad would take me on weekends, we'd go to the diner, I'd stay overnight, and he'd bring me home the next day. With one blink, things began to change. I would soon realize not all parental bonds are what they are *supposed to be*. Subconsciously, I was being thrown into insecurity and a shaky foundation, because the most important male in my life was about to abandon me. I quickly learned the meaning of conditional.

He met his new wife and our visits became a lot less frequent. I remember one particular weekend he was supposed to pick me up, I was waiting at the door with my overnight bag packed. And he never came …

Soon, our visits dwindled and then stopped completely. He went on to adopt two daughters and moved away from his old life as he settled into his new role as "their" dad.

I would spend the next thirty-five years wondering HOW he could leave me. And WHY?

That experience kick-started a chain of life events that made me question the authenticity of the human soul. I lost trust in the world and sought safety as I neared adulthood.

I moved out of my house just one month before my eighteenth birthday to live with my very best friend. I was determined to make a life for myself. My mom and stepdad and siblings moved the same month to New Hampshire for a business opportunity, and I decided to stay.

WHY? It was safe. After all, I grew up in New York, and I needed that anchor of everything I knew and felt comfortable with—especially because there was this deep, dark sadness in my soul, which I can only assume was due to the loss of my father. I felt an indescribable emptiness, but I stuck with my plan because I needed to feel safety even if it was to create my own.

My dream was to become a teacher in the town I grew up in and make a difference in the lives of children. It was a loving job, and I hoped it would fill the hole in my heart (that hole that was hard to put into words, that yearning for something but not quite knowing what that something was). You know, *that* hole.

I turned to bartending (not knowing what the heck I was doing) to make ends meet. Those poor customers were so darn patient. They would eventually change their drink of choice to bottled beer, because they knew that was a safe bet with me behind the bar. In my own defense, I did get better with time. I spent the next few years putting myself through undergrad classes to get my teaching degree.

Things were unfolding just as I had planned. I even stumbled upon love!

My first husband was the epitome of strength. He was a go-getter. He was determined and protective and made me feel safe. We got married young, and go figure: I married the man who was everything my biological father wasn't. We were together ten years. I had that white picket fence and a stable job I was passionate about. We brought our beautiful firstborn into the world. I had just graduated with my master's degree, and I had this beautiful baby boy and a husband who worked hard. We had a good life according to what things were *supposed to be.*

Lesson learned! You *can* change your views and values based on who you are becoming. You don't need to be stuck in the past. It's time to figure out who you were before the world told you who you were *supposed to be*.

So I want you to ask yourself a question right this very second: Was the beginning of your adulthood predetermined by your childhood circumstances?

Message for the soul: When things don't work out as you had hoped, it's the end of the chapter—not the end of the book.

• • • • •

Chapter Two

Things Aren't What They Seem

M ost of us tend to paint our world as perfect for those on the outside. You may be unfulfilled and empty in your marriage, your career—your *life*. BUT you tend to hide behind a persona of perfection. Especially in this day and age where social media is so prevalent, it's easy to portray yourself any way you want and hide behind the computer.

Are things as happy as you make them out to be, really?

In my opinion, true happiness doesn't come from a fancy car or huge home. It doesn't come from designer bags or a fierce pair of red-bottomed heels. (Although, I did get a pair of those notorious heels as my fortieth birthday gift to myself, and they DO make me smile.) I'm giggling as I write that, because I have been a shopaholic all my life. I was totally guilty of painting the world rosy, and I turned to being an obsessive consumer because my emptiness *consumed* me. I hoped to fill that void and try to find "happiness." That consumption was amazing for the moment, I'll give you that, but it was all instant gratification. And instant gratification fades quickly. After the fade, what are you left with? Yourself!

Happiness is an inside job. It's something that is a direct reflection of living your purpose, following your dreams, and loving yourself enough to seek the good and avoid the bad. Happiness has depth. It's something that stems from the soul and isn't a mood. It's a way of life.

Why must you walk with the weight of the world on your shoulders and feel pressured to make your hunched shoulders look like pretty, weightless, sparkly fairy wings?

The answer is simple: YOU DON'T KNOW ANY OTHER WAY!

Unless you have established your lack of purpose and fulfillment and happiness, you can't move forward. That's why it often takes a trauma, a death, a diagnosis, or a job loss to smack you in the face and make you aware that something needs to change. Unless you intentionally work on yourself and grow your mind to see what else is out there, you will always be stuck—stuck in that trap of what things are *supposed to be*.

Like most, my divorce was devastating. It made me question trust and drained my spirit. I remember lying in bed one night and asking myself, "If today was my last day, would I be happy with that?" The answer was NO! I knew I was capable of more. I was finally realizing I had the power to choose what to accept and what to release. I was choosing to release what everyone else thought my life should look like, which forced me into some serious self-examination.

It's like when you take a shower and there's all that condensation on the mirror. If you keep the door closed, that fog lasts a whole lot longer than it does if you open the door.

Think about how that foggy bathroom feels after a while—you may feel overheated, like you can't breathe and you're suffocating. Well, it's the same with life: Once you "open the door" and let in some light, energy, and new perspective, the mirror begins to clear. You begin to see yourself again and feel how much lighter the air is. Everything returns to a comfortable state. My point is that you don't know what you don't know. If you are feeling stuck in a routine or job or marriage or friendship or living situation that is not serving you, something needs to change.

I'm not saying go get a divorce or leave your job. I'm simply suggesting you open that bathroom door, even if it's just a little crack, so you can see and feel things in a different way. Sometimes, you're stuck in your own head and can be your own worst enemy. There are so many resources out there to help; you just don't always know it because you haven't been open to it.

One of the "go-to" things I have found very helpful is practicing some kind of personal development every single day. I'm not talking about starting it and then giving it up once you feel better. I mean do something every single day that will make YOU a better version of YOU! Isn't that an awesome concept?

Making yourself a priority and learning a little bit each day will keep that door open to new possibilities. And, most importantly, it gives you hope! Read a self-help book. I'm really big on those. I believe in them so wholeheartedly, I wrote one for dang sake (wink, wink)! Try listening to a documentary, or go see a motivational speaker. Better yet, YouTube it! There are tons of short, inspiring clips you can Google, and tailor it to whatever you need at the moment. Meditate! Take the time to quiet your mind and relax your body. It is incredible what a few, deep, mindful breaths can do!

Whatever you do, don't stay closed in that foggy, stuffy, uncomfortable bathroom. The world is such a breath of fresh air, and you just need to open that door— even if it's just a crack!

Lesson learned! Take the time to grow yourself every single day. Personal development is a vital part of your maturity, success, and happiness. It's an ongoing process of understanding and developing, so you can become the very best version of yourself.

Ask yourself: Are you open to using the resources around you? Are you willing to open that door to change the things that you're unhappy with?

Message for the soul: "If nothing changes, nothing changes. If you keep on doing what you're doing, you're going to keep on getting what you're getting. You want change, make some."

—Courtney C. Stevens,
The Lies About Truth

• • • • •

Chapter Three

Delayed Perfection

Although simply stated, this Chinese proverb can be very profound: "The person who moves a mountain begins by carrying small stones."

Think about what that means. Every obstacle, difficult decision, or trying situation is leading you to great things. With every roadblock, you are led toward the best version of yourself. Now, truthfully speaking, some people never see past the difficulty. They find it easier to view hard times as being handed a bad deck of cards or just having crappy luck. Seeing past the difficulty itself is the part that takes INTENTION.

As I explained in the last chapter, growing your mind will help you broaden your outlook. Instead of just seeing the situation for what it is, you will learn how to see the whole picture and what life is trying to teach you. Every last experience is molding you, shaping you into something really amazing. *You* have the ability to see that glass as half empty or half full. I don't know about you, but if I were stuck in the desert and stumbled across half a glass of aqua, you can bet your bottom dollar I would NOT be complaining that I was only able to hydrate a little. I'd be thanking my lucky stars that I had liquid to sustain me, even if only for a short while. There is a clear decision to make when faced with anything: Will you choose gratitude?

This is where your growth continues. Adversity is leading you toward happiness, but are you open to accepting the lessons? Or are you shut down, because you see the glass as half empty? It's not something that will happen overnight. It takes time and careful refinement. Enlightenment is a magical process. If you're open to it, the process will continue to serve you all your life. It's like a *delayed perfection*—a gift that will just keep on giving if your heart is open.

Nothing will ever be perfect. I don't think "perfection" exists, but I believe you can make your own happiness and create your own version of what perfect means to you. The process leads you. If you are willing to let go of the life you had planned, you can invite in the life that is awaiting you.

Your existence is not a clear-cut path. Just when things feel like they are going smoothly, the universe reminds you that life will throw curve balls to keep pushing you forward. It places circumstances in your way to see just how strong you are. It can force you to build your character, or it can push you to self-destruct. The choice is yours. You were not meant to coast. You were meant to thrive. Whether or not you do is up to you.

So there I was—twenty-eight years old, separated from my husband and going through the logistics of divorce. I was the mom of a toddler and knee-deep in the terrible twos. I was saddened by my divorce and, most days, I felt I had failed.

Should I have worked harder at mending the things that ailed our unity? Over time, I would ask myself that question and an overwhelming sense of energy would come over me—something that almost took my breath away. It was bright white (if you can picture an energy being a color) light. It was such a powerful feeling. It reassured me that it was all going to be OK, and it overtook me. This new phase of life was going to allow me to experience more of what I deserved. It would allow me to see a different path—rather than be so stuck in what things were *supposed to be*. This energy began to lighten my heart, which had felt so heavy. I started to view the world as a place of opportunity and wonder. The sky looked bluer. The sun shined brighter, and I realized there was more out there for me.

Like a breath of fresh air one day, I met someone new. It was the first time in ten years I was open to noticing a man other than my ex-husband. In walks this Physical Education teacher, who was a leave replacement for the year at the school I worked in. I took notice of how tall he was. He had a strong presence and was very athletic-looking—the complete opposite of what my "type" of guy typically looked like. Something about him intrigued me. I got butterflies when I saw him. I had extra pep in my step when he was around. What started as a silly little mutual crush turned into so much more!

It's amazing what can happen when you break the chains that bind you. I learned that being open to change can feel good. (Great, actually!) It doesn't have to be scary and unsafe. Depending on how you decide to look at it, change can be quite beautiful and refreshing. It can rejuvenate a stale spirit and leave you completely invigorated!

This new beau and I quickly fell head over heels for one another. He was a family man and had a strong work ethic. He proved to love my son just as much as he loved me. Together, we slowly meshed our lives over the next two years. He proposed to me in June 2008, and we got married two months later in an intimate garden ceremony. It was magical! We bought our first home together and gave birth to the most gentle little baby boy. With two boys, a passionate and loving marriage, amazing jobs, and a modest home that was ours, life was our version of happy!

For the first time in my life, I felt truly content and safe. I knew he would take care of my heart forever and never abandon me.

I remember when I was younger, during long car rides I'd gaze up into the sky and think to myself, "Somewhere under this big, blue sky is the man I will spend forever with!" And I found him!

I felt like life was perfection. It was our own version of it. It felt kinda like the glass that's half full, but now it's filled all the way to the tippy top. That is the feeling he gives me. Funny enough, we are actually *imperfectly perfect* together. We are so different, yet so much the same. I am the emotionally driven, spiritual, enthusiastic, short-fused one who goes after everything I want. My husband is calm, quiet, reserved, emotionally guarded, and gentle. Despite our differences, he is the yin to my yang, and I love him for loving me so faithfully. For the first time in my life, a man is truly showing me what love looks like—with no stipulations or conditions.

Even all these years later, I still smile when I see his name pop up on my phone. He will be my old-and-gray partner. I envision us in our eighties, sitting in rocking chairs as we listen to the ocean from our dream house.

It may not have been the life that was *supposed to be*, but I followed my heart, which lead me directly toward where I was meant to be.

Lesson learned! It is delayed perfection!

Sometimes "change" is mandatory. The secret to being open to it is to focus all your energy on building the new, not fighting the old! Stop looking for happiness in the same place you lost it. If life requires a shift, believe in it. Let it take you wherever you are meant to go.

If you follow your heart and put any fear you have into a box and close it, you can feel confident you will be guided safely.

Ask yourself: Are you willing to close the doors that are no longer serving you or your life, so you can make room for new ones to open?

Message for the soul: Sometimes you don't know the weight of something you've been carrying until you feel the relief of its release.

● ● ● ● ●

Chapter 4

Bumps, Detours and Potholes

"An optimist understands that life can
be a bumpy road, but at least it is leading
somewhere. They learn from mistakes and
failures, and are not afraid to fail again."
—Harvey Mackay

Rest assured that just when life seems to be going smoothly, the universe will put something in your way so you can learn your next lesson.

Let me back up a bit: We wanted a baby. After a few months of marriage, we found out we were expecting our first child together. It was a dream come true. We were in love and about to bring a product of that into the world. We gave birth to our second son and quickly decided we wanted a third child. Within a year, we tried again. (After all, I was getting up there in age, and I didn't want any complications if I could avoid them.)

This time it wasn't so easy. We tried for a year and realized something was wrong. I had never had an issue with fertility before, so this was unchartered territory for us. Each passing month—each negative pregnancy test—chipped away at our spirits.

Have you ever felt like you want something so badly, but it's just outside your reach? One of the worst feelings ever, right? That's because we are conditioned to expect instant gratification in life. But it doesn't always work that way, now does it?

It's hard to understand *why* when you are in that disappointment, but it's the universe's way of paving your path. Through the frustration and disappointment, it's leading you toward where you will ultimately end up—where you belong—and at exactly the RIGHT time, even though it may not be according to what you want or expect.

A regimented person like me didn't see that back then. I got frustrated, tense, sad, and angry. I was shut down to the lesson I should have been open to learning. Instead, I focused on "the problem." So guess what? The universe gave me even more tests—three to be exact. (I guess it was with the hope that I would finally be open to learning what I was meant to learn.)

We saw a fertility specialist and, finally, we were pregnant! We were overflowing with joy! Finally, we would feel complete!

It felt like we were cruising down a new, nicely paved highway. Wind was blowing in our hair (insert the song: Ride Like The Wind by Christopher Cross here). Before the next song could play, we hit what felt like the world's biggest pothole. One that we hit so hard, it popped the tire instantly!

At nine weeks, we lost the baby. I was actually administering the state exams for my third-grade students when I realized I was miscarrying. Our hearts were heavy with our loss. I remember making a cup of tea and wrapping myself in a blanket and just sobbing, thinking to myself, "WHY? Why us? We're good people. Why?"

The reason, which we see very clearly now, was that God had a plan for us. He wanted us to use our struggle to help others. That realization came to me like an epiphany! I started to share bits and pieces of our struggles on social media with the hope that our experience could help people get through their losses.

I felt like my struggle had a purpose, and that was the beginning of my effort to use my experiences to help other people. In a matter of three years, we lost three pregnancies—one was a set of twins.

I remember the last loss most vividly. I went in for my checkup. We had just heard the baby's strong heartbeat the week prior. I was so excited to see that little dot on the screen and hear the beautiful sound of LIFE inside my belly. I just craved that feeling of motherhood again.

There I was on the exam table, eager and beaming with excitement. The doctor was quiet.

The Doppler was eerily silent.

My world suddenly got cold.

It was as if I were out of my own body when the doctor said, "I'm sorry. There is no heartbeat."

It had happened again … I couldn't wait to get off that table! I just wanted to crawl up under the covers in my bed and disappear. Inspiring others was the last thing on my mind.

I felt like I was being punished for something. It was like a bad dream. All we wanted was to love another child. Why was it so hard?

But life is not meant to be rushed. What is meant for YOU takes time. Some of your greatest lessons are learned through the worst of times. It's almost like an earthquake that rattles your foundation just enough to force you to start fixing those cracks in it.

Lesson learned! A man who is a master of patience understands the value in what there is to come. Having patience keeps your mind and heart open. It's the gift of being able to see past the emotion.

Ask yourself: If you fell seven times, would you get up for an eighth?

Message for the Soul: When life's road has potholes and speed bumps, it makes you a better driver! Don't confuse a detour for a stop sign!

• • • • •

Chapter 5

Difficult Roads and Beautiful Destinations

"What if I fall?"
"Oh, but my darling, What if you fly?"
—Erin Hanson

It's one of my favorite sayings, and it would carry me through this difficult decade of my life and beyond.

How will you know if you don't try?

The next few months were hard. My husband and I questioned God and our faith. We couldn't comprehend why we were being dealt these cards. *This* was the first time I could actually see that life can be really difficult and adversity is a reality. Some people have bigger mountains to climb; nonetheless, a mountain is a mountain! When you are emotionally beaten down, it's hard to muster the strength to keep trucking up those tall terrains.

This is where that intention comes into play.

When life hands you lemons, you have a very clear-cut choice: Are you going to pucker and scowl from the bitter taste, or will you throw those yellow bad boys into a gorgeous clear pitcher and make some delicious lemonade?

There's something really intriguing about getting knocked down and then mustering the confidence to get back up again. I almost feel like it is life's way of taunting my character. It's the universe testing my strength to see if I will give up or stand taller than ever.

Wallowing in a sad situation does nothing. I'm not saying it's not important to FEEL what you need to FEEL. I am telling you, "DON'T WALLOW!"

Quite frankly, people have their own lives happening. Do you really think they want to hear the same sob story over and over again? If you wallow, it's like a broken record. Soon, it becomes white noise to the outside world. I know it seems harsh, but it's the raw, unfiltered truth. It's up to YOU to make life what you want it to be!

After a few months of mourning our last loss, my husband and I made a decision. We were going to make a final try to become parents for a third time. It was THAT important to us. Together, we came up with a plan for our last attempt. We prepared ourselves for the worst but envisioned only the best. If it didn't happen, we understood we'd need to accept whatever direction this took us.

We just about drained our savings account and committed to one round of in vitro fertilization. It wasn't covered by insurance, so we knew this was it! If it didn't happen, we would have to let it go and enjoy the blessings we already had.

Around this time, I began to read about the power of visualization. It's an amazing tool for your tool belt. The more you get your mind to believe what you want, the more likely it is to happen—and that is a fact. That little saying "mind over matter" has a whole lotta truth in it!

Imagine that. Can it be true that you "picture something" and it will come true? Heck yeah!

Mental imaging has been around for years. Some of the most successful people use this technique to help them succeed. Without getting too technical, scientists have determined that paths of interconnected nerve cells link what the body does to the brain impulses that control the body.

We had two sons, so I began to picture a daughter. I would be grateful for whatever gender God blessed us with, but if I were envisioning my desired outcome, why not picture the daughter I'd always dreamed of having?

In my head, she was beautiful with long dark hair. She had a powerful presence and a confidence that made people stop in their tracks. She would be my best friend and have our boys wrapped around her little finger.

I began to go to acupuncture to help my body prepare for the egg retrieval. During my sessions, I'd close my eyes and visualize the blood flow to my belly stimulating healthy, strong eggs. After the transfer, I pictured the embryo adhering to me, its mommy, and begin to thrive.

Two weeks after our last procedure, we found out we were pregnant. On my thirty-fifth birthday, we reached twelve weeks, and we realized it was happening! It worked—flipping our minds from wallowing in our sadness to being proactive worked!

Nine months later, we delivered our perfect baby girl. She was everything I had imagined her to be—and then some. Our three-year infertility battle led us to the most amazing honor, raising our one and only baby girl, V. As I write this book years later, she continues to fill our lives with more joy than we can express in words.

She is certainly our "beautiful destination!"

Lesson learned! Your intention creates your reality. It is where you focus your energy that matters. The secret of changing your life is setting intentions. A wish, a dream, a goal is just *that*—a wish, a dream, a goal. They can be left untouched if you don't CHOOSE to go after them and put action behind HOW you are going to do that. There must be intention and focused energy behind any desired outcome.

Ask yourself: Will you wallow, or will you rise?

Message for the soul: "There are two primary choices in life: to accept conditions as they exist, or accept the responsibility for changing them."

—Denis Waitley

• • • • •

Chapter 6

Warrior Status

Y ou are so much stronger than you think!
Each and every one of you was built to rock this life "thing." Strength is something that is exercised with each hurdle you face. With every year that passes, your experiences bring you closer and closer to where you are meant to be. With every pain, you become more empathetic and more caring. You emerge a deeper, more understanding version of yourself. You have the ability to appreciate the miracle of life.

Just before V's second birthday, we had a beautiful Christmas dinner that our family hosted for the first time. We were in the spirit of the season, enjoying twinkling holiday lights and warm, comforting foods. We were creating some new holiday traditions, and my husband and I had never been happier. We felt so complete—so whole! We looked forward to raising our three beautiful, nutty children.

The world was at our fingertips. Things were finally smooth—even-keeled—and we could just enjoy all God had blessed us with!

Then came January 15, 2015. It's a day that will forever be engrained in my soul. I remember getting excited about V's second birthday party, and I was so happy because it was a snow day! I had some free time at home to put together the final touches for her special day. I was on the phone with my sister-in-law and had a warm cup of coffee in hand. My other hand happened to graze over my neck.

"What the hell is that?!" I thought.

It was a lump the size of a golf ball. And at that moment, I knew. I knew life was never going to be the same, and a few short days later, my intuition became a reality.

I had Stage 3S cancer. I was diagnosed with Hodgkin's Lymphoma. The cancer had invaded my neck and chest, and it began to enter my spleen.

At the moment of diagnosis, I couldn't breathe. I didn't know if I was going to live or die. My babies ... my husband ...

No one can ever prepare you for the words, "You have cancer."

It was like the rug had been ripped out from under us. We lost our footing and our faces were slammed to the ground. Our spirits felt bruised and battered. The infertility created some small cracks in our foundation. But CANCER—that crack was so big that we questioned whether or not our footing would ever be stable again.

Twelve torturous rounds of chemo became our new normal. We took two-hour car rides every other week to have poison administered into my body. I lost my hair, my eyelashes, my energy, my vibrant spirit ...

Cancer knocked me to my knees and had me begging for mercy. There were some days where I held my rosary beads and pleaded for God to have mercy on me. Each treatment buried me deeper and deeper into darkness—a darkness I had never experienced before. I turned to my faith to help lift me out. I would sit in our empty church and sob, begging God to allow me to SEE what He was trying to teach me. I knew it was another lesson, but I needed clarity to understand it.

I began to share my everyday reality on my social media page, "Kelley's Journey." It's a closed Facebook group where anyone who wants to follow along can request access. It became an outlet, a way for me to feel connected to life and get the love and support I so desperately needed. Those days were so dark. Writing soothed even the most painful moments.

I began thinking more and more about my nutrition and exercised almost every day. It was gentle yoga, but it got my body moving and my endorphins going, and *that* in turn helped my spirit.

Faith, family, friends, food, and fun—those were the five key components to my success and healing. The dark skies began to lift and out came the sun. I found myself prioritizing life, seizing more days, and trying my damnedest to make the most of moments. There was a powerful fire within me that was beginning to burn brightly. I decided to grab this disease by the _____ (you fill in the blank) and take our life back. After all, wallowing will get you nowhere, right?

I was a wife, a mother, and a warrior! I was ready and willing to take this fight head-on, titanium style, and that's exactly what I did.

Six months and twelve rounds of chemo later, I was declared CANCER-FREE!

I not only accepted the title Survivor, but I took on a self-proclaimed Warrior status, too, which I now pass on to each of my fellow fighters.

My mind began to take that title very seriously, and I was determined not to be defeated!

Lesson learned! Believe in yourself. One of the strongest factors for success is self-esteem. Believe that you can do it, believe that you deserve it, and believe that you can get it!

Ask yourself: Are the explosions in your life pushing you, or crushing you?

Message for the soul: A splintered soul can find solace.

"A bird sitting on a tree is never afraid of the branch breaking, because her trust is not on the branch but on her own wings."

—Unknown

• • • • •

Chapter 7

With One Blink

In the blink of an eye, everything can change. It's one of those sayings people post on social media or throw around in conversation, but stop and really think about how true those words are. In one second, something amazing can happen, and in another ... something really tragic. We just don't know what the future holds, so being happy is of the utmost importance.

Big life events are notorious for unveiling new perspectives and a different outlook on LIFE. They allow you to reflect on where you are currently and evaluate whether or not you are satisfied with that. Those reflections then help guide some important tweaks and necessary refinements.

Well, cancer was IT for me. After all, I slipped past death. I was so thankful to be alive that I felt I needed to give back to thank God for allowing me to LIVE! I started to get involved with the cancer community and support others—even if it was just to give advice about how to get through chemo or just to lend an ear. I also started an online support group. I literally dove into a desperate feeling of wanting to save the world. I thought that was my role. It felt like my purpose was to help others. After all, I had to give thanks for being alive, right?

I quickly realized, instead of dealing with the trauma of cancer, I masked what I was feeling by diving into helping others. Little did I know how important it was to help myself. As much as I wanted to seize those moments and feel calm, I had a constant internal battle with myself.

What was the problem?

Why was my spirit in constant turmoil?

After all, I was alive! What more could I want?

I began to take a very close look inward. I started to see that my whole life, I gave and gave and gave—until I finally gave away my health. It may sound strange to hear that, but it's true. All my life, I have been hypersensitive to the needs and feelings of others—most of the time, to a fault. I internalized every argument and cross look. If someone was upset, I'd make it my duty to help them feel better, no matter what I needed to do. I lived for other people and put my needs on the back burner.

And *with one blink*, I had CANCER!

Eventually, it catches up to you.

Let's be honest; NO SINGLE PERSON can truly save the world. But you can save yourself and the light you bring! The world needs more light, so in this chapter I want to stress the importance of self-love.

What does it mean to really love yourself? Is it a manicure and pedicure to pamper yourself? Well, maybe … But it's really much bigger than that. It's taking the time to accept yourself without judgment. It's freeing yourself from the burden of needing acceptance from others. It's learning how and when you need to make time for yourself and feeling OK when you do.

I know, I know—insert excuses here:

But my kids have …

But I need to do …

But there's a deadline of …

I can't because …

Who has the time?

We are all chock-full of excuses! Why fight so hard to put everything else in front of your own needs? Is it that you were programed about how things are *supposed to be?* Maybe that's it. You think you have to fit into this mold.

I'm here to tell you, "NO!" Loving yourself isn't a courtesy. It's a necessity!

Guess what? That laundry, your kids, your spouse, your work, that dust on the coffee table—they are all part of your everyday grind. Yes, they need to be tended to; I'm simply suggesting you carve out some time for yourself.

If you put yourself on top of your to-do list every day, the rest of life will fall into place. It allows you to fuel up and be the best version of yourself you can possibly be. Think about it like this: How long can a car run on empty? It's only a matter of time before that car will stop and be unable to move. The same goes for us as human beings. If you live to work, make money, maintain a household, and keep the people around you happy, where do you fit into the equation?

You don't!

And when you are not anywhere in that equation on a daily basis, your car eventually runs out of gas because you didn't fuel it. Nothing can run on fumes! Believe me, I've already tested that scenario. When you are on empty, the result can be a physical issue—like feeling fatigued or getting sick. An empty tank also can lead to mental burnout, depression, and anxiety.

The point is that it's impossible to live a truly fulfilled, happy life without making yourself a priority. It's not selfish; it's necessary! You must not neglect yourself. How can you be the best parent, spouse, professional, or friend if you aren't the best version of yourself first?

So here's the deal: Love your damn self, people!

Love yourself enough to be respectful and accepting of your feelings, and be gentle on the days you need it.

Love yourself enough to TAKE ACTION for your happiness.

Love yourself enough to set boundaries and say NO when you need to—without the feeling of guilt.

Love yourself enough to do things that make you happy. Just because you're a mom or dad doesn't mean you can't get out those dancing shoes and let your hair down once in a while.

Love yourself enough to be physically active each day. Those endorphins feel amazing, and YOU DESERVE THAT!

Love yourself enough to carefully select the right foods for your body. When your body gets what it needs, it runs optimally.

Love yourself enough to be surrounded by people who lift you higher and challenge you.

My favorite one: Love yourself enough to eliminate toxic people and relationships.

Here's a side note on that: Drama is everywhere! It's so debilitating to a healthy spirit and does a number on your emotional well-being. So remember: Other people's crap is other people's crap.

You can be a good friend to people without letting them manipulate or treat you badly. You also need to be a good friend to yourself. Accept nothing less than healthy, reciprocal relationships, because THAT is what you deserve. The more you learn about yourself, the more you can figure out what you're willing to tolerate and who you're willing to tolerate it from.

If you continue to teach others how to treat you by setting boundaries and communicating respectfully, the more you will find yourself escaping those dramatic relationships. There's a huge difference in the way you feel if you fly with the go-getters, well-wishers, and rock stars. Chances are they will display unconditional love and want success for you—and you will have NO DRAMA! God knows who belongs in your life. Be open to closing doors when doors need to be closed, so you can be led to another door that's meant for you to open!

The idea of self-care and love can be misunderstood. It doesn't always mean going to the spa to get pampered. It means trusting your heart and intuition to guide you in life. It means taking the time to listen to your heart often. Sometimes it means being able to say no to something, because it will overwhelm you to take on one more responsibility. Sometimes self-care is knowing what will support you and what will drain you. Talking about self-care is easy, but believing you are worthy of it is often quite challenging. Practicing this everyday, though will bring peace into your life, and the benefits are compounding.

As you are reading this book, I'm hoping your life hasn't brought you down a deep, dark road. But if it has, you do not have to stay stuck in that darkness. There is hope, and you can get yourself out. You are worthy of love.

Lesson learned! YOU matter. Love yourself so intensely that it shows others how to do it. Put yourself on the top of your to-do list every single day, and the rest will fall right into place.

Ask yourself: What do you do to show yourself love each day? (If you don't like the answer—lucky you—it's an easy fix!)

Message for the soul: "Perhaps we should love ourselves so fiercely, that when others see us they know exactly how it should be done."

—Rudy Francisco

• • • • •

Chapter 8

Another Mountain

Just when things start going in the right direction—SURPRISE—there's another mountain to climb!

Life is an endless process of growth and discovering yourself. How boring would it be if things were always easy? Trials and tribulations are meant to lead us and challenge us. I'd be willing to bet everyone in the world has something they've battled. Whether you rise or fall depends on what you do with that mountain. Will you grab your hiking boots and walking stick, or will you allow it to defeat you before you even attempt the hike?

You are meant to thrive in this life—not just exist.

Learning from what has gone wrong will help you grow. If you allow your eyes to be open, it will guide you to a life of pure bliss where every day is filled with so much joy that it actually feels like a vacation! Can you imagine a life where (despite what hell you've gone through) you can't wait to wake up each morning and live it? Do you want your heart to smile from within the deepest part of your being? It is possible. You can recover from hard times and emerge a happier, more harmonious version of yourself. Life CAN be enriching and completely fulfilling.

You can make your own version of perfect! In 2017, I was almost two years cancer-free. I was turning forty and this milestone year was going to be a huge celebration. After all, I'd been through hell and back, and I couldn't wait to start a new decade and put it all behind me. I planned a huge fortieth birthday bash with sixty of my closest friends and family. The theme was pink!

Pink, pink, pink—I was completely addicted to the color and needed it everywhere. Pink is so sexy and fabulous. It can be soft or fierce, depending on the shade. It is such a parallel to my personality, and, yes, I accept myself enough to have just written that! It's something I've finally embraced, and there's nothing more freeing than having confidence in what makes you uniquely *you*.

That night was one of the most special nights of my life. We ate, we danced, we reminisced, and we laughed. The party was almost perfect. I wore the most gorgeous pair of shoes. They were royal blue with lots of bling on the heel. They made me feel feminine, beautiful, striking, and strong all at the same time.

Looking back, I'm so happy I had that night, because the rug was about to be pulled out from under our feet again. It would leave us face-first on the ground, staring at fear.

Did I mention that a few weeks before my birthday, I went for a routine mammogram and ultrasound, which picked up NOTHING? (Yay, right?) I happened to have a very diligent doctor who decided to send me for a more extensive test, which ultimately saved my life by detecting BREAST CANCER.

Yes, you read correctly. I had cancer—again.

We were in the mall (the night before my actual fortieth) when we found out, and my children witnessed the diagnosis. It was the lowest point of my life, and it was in front of my babies. For a fleeting moment, all the "there's-a-reason-for-everything" crap went out the window! We were shocked, angry, defeated, and sad. Our family felt slammed, again.

Our faces hit the pavement at what felt like 100 miles an hour. My milestone and our new beginning, that fresh start and decade that was supposed to be all ours, our time to leave pain in the past and start to rebuild as a family … Well, God had a different plan for us. I had a lot more learning and growing to do, and this was how He was going to do the teaching.

I lost my breasts. I lost all my reproductive organs. I felt like I was losing everything that made me … me! I lost some friends and people I thought loved me unconditionally. Ultimately, I felt lost! I was completely and utterly lost in the dark, stormy tornado called cancer.

It has been a conscious effort this time around to remind myself that I am not my cancer. After all, when this is all you've known for several years, it's easy to lose your identity and become a victim. I constantly remind myself that I'm a mom, a wife, a friend, and a teacher. I'm a daughter, niece, dancer, and singer. I love to laugh and be near the water. I write to empty (and fill) my heart and express my truths for people to learn from and gain happiness and perspective!

It's easy to view adversity as a thief, stealing happiness from your existence, but it's actually quite the opposite. When the fog clears and you can think straight, if you are open to it, you can see adversity is a blessing that gives you the gift of a new outlook—one that you would never be able to fathom without some sort of compromising situation.

So as I sit here and write this book, I am in the midst of my breast-cancer fight. This time around, I realize (even more so) the importance of truly making myself a priority. I began to do some research to understand the correlation between my two cancers. The doctors said they were unrelated, but I knew there had to be a common denominator.

Do you know who that dirty little culprit was? Stress! All that people-pleasing, putting others first, and smiling all the time just to make everyone else feel good *caught up to me.*

Unresolved resentment, angst, worry, and anger will put your immune system on the back burner. It will literally eat away at your body. The great news is there are so many amazing ways to help eliminate stress from your life. I'm a huge proponent of dealing with the emotional correlation to disease.

I need to make my emotional health my top priority. We all must learn to F.L.Y. (first love yourself). There was a particular day just recently when I had a flashback: I saw myself as a little girl, and I realized *she* was counting on *me* to protect her.

When the mind starts to think you've had enough, your heart reminds you not to give up. Life is a story really. You write it and the editing process never seems to end. You are constantly evolving and getting ready for the next lesson. With each passing year, you learn, grow, and improve. With each storm, it deepens your roots and shows you exactly what you are capable of. It allows you to see the indomitable will deep within your soul. Will you take this and be bitter, or will you use it to get better? The choice is always yours!

So when you are down-and-out, I want you to write a letter to your "sad self." Try to be as raw and honest as possible and get it out onto paper. Use this as a form of emptying the soul of anything heavy and releasing it into the universe.

Here's an example of what a "sad self" letter can look like.

Dear Sad Self,

Today I feel alone. Feeling misunderstood in the outside world is becoming a more standard thought process, which is stifling my emotions. While everyone else is going on with their lives, I feel stuck here in the darkness of my thoughts. The air I'm breathing feels thick and sooty. Sharing my feelings with anyone scares me, because I feel like I'll be misunderstood and judged as ungrateful or negative. There is so much swirling around like a tornado in my mind, and the storm doesn't stop. I want to see the sunshine, yet, I don't know how.

Those I should be able to depend on have different priorities, and I feel abandoned. This feeling brings me back to unresolved childhood issues, and I don't like to feel that. So I stuff the feelings down deep and slap a smile on my face, so everyone else thinks I'm OK. After all, it's easier to say everything is FINE than to deal with rejection. Hopefully, tomorrow will be a better day, and I'll feel better soon.

Love,
Me

It's your turn. Use the lines below and take a few minutes to write your own letter. The release of negative emotions is key to overcoming adversity and healing from a difficult time in your life.

· ·

· ·

· ·

· ·

· ·

· ·

· ·

· ·

· ·

· ·

· ·

· ·

· ·

· ·

· ·

· ·

Now that you've written your "sad self" letter, read it to yourself. Allow yourself to FEEL all of the emotions as you read each and every pure and raw emotional word. Cry your eyes out if that's where your body is taking you. Yell at the top of your lungs if your heart takes you there. The point is to feel it and release it. You are safe here, and stuffing your emotions won't change anything. You picked up this book for a reason. Remember Courtney C. Stevens' quote, "If nothing changes, nothing changes."

Now take a deep, cleansing breath. All of those feelings and thoughts which were swirling around in your head are now out of your body. It's released ...

Now that all the heaviness is on the paper, it's time to flip your mindset. Take those feelings and reverse them. A huge part of the healing process is mindset, and you know I wasn't about to let you get away with wallowing in your crap, right?!

It's time to use your "sad self" letter to write a letter of hope. You will greet your "hopeful self" this time.

It's important that you use positive words only. Think about your desired outcome and use that to fuel the flow of your thoughts.

Here's an example:

Dear Hopeful Self,

Today, I feel hopeful. I'm feeling like the world is truly at my fingertips, and my heart is open to all the positivity life has to offer. I deserve happiness and peace in my heart. Everyone around me is living their lives, and I am embracing all the magical moments in mine. I'm not focusing to the left or right of me. My eyes are locked on all that awaits ME.

I will express my feelings in a graceful way and accept people's reactions as they are, without internalizing those reactions as a reflection of me. My mind is clear and focused, and I imagine a bright white light following me wherever I go. I am protected by the universe and safe. I smile from my heart and want to share that with as many people as I possibly can today. I love myself enough to accept who I am with pride. I will continue to grow and learn. I can't wait to see what TODAY has in store for me.

Love,
Me

Wow! What a different message. When you flip your mindset, you have the ability to change your mood from deep and dark to light and airy. The trick is that it needs to be intentional.

Now you know what I'm going to ask you to do. You got it! Go ahead and write that new letter to your "hopeful self" and see how darn awesome you feel afterward.

· ·

· ·

· ·

· ·

· ·

· ·

· ·

· ·

· ·

· ·

· ·

· ·

· ·

· ·

· ·

· ·

· ·

· ·

Lesson learned! It's OK to feel sadness, anger, or disappointment. But you must flip that mindset if you want to move past it. Life will happen and emotions (even those negative emotions) are healthy, but it's important not to stay stuck!

Ask yourself: Do you put everyone else before yourself? If the answer is yes, list some ways you will put your emotional needs first.

Do you put too much emphasis on the opinions of others? Or do you love yourself enough to accept them and their behaviors without letting that negativity seep in?

Message for the soul:

Dear You,
Make peace with the mirror and watch your reflection change!
Love, Kelley
XOXO

. . . . .

Chapter 9

Food for the Soul

There has been so much talk about the emotional "self," but do you realize the positive effects food can make on your life? You know that old saying, "You are what you eat." Well, it's true! If you eat junk, you feel like junk. If you fuel your body with wholesome, clean foods, your body will thank you by running optimally. Proper nutrition can give you energy, make your skin glow, and allow you to simply *feel* the gift of a healthy body.

Most of the time, people complain they don't have the time to commit to healthy eating and some form of exercise. Yet, we all know how good it is for us. Why does it take so much effort to do what we know is best for the one and only body we have to live in?

We are beautifully composed of millions and millions of tiny cells. Each and every one of those cells serves a distinct purpose, protecting you and replenishing itself. Unfortunately, in this day and age, even if you think you are eating healthy, chances are you are not doing even half of what your body needs. The problem is the foods and products that are offered to consumers are shiny, bright, and wrapped in pretty little packages that look so appealing it's hard to resist them. The reality is most foods and everyday products are processed and preserved. This makes your body work overtime to get rid of the ingredients that make those products look and taste good and last as long as they do on the shelves.

As a result of my recent health battles, I've become an advocate of a well-balanced diet, especially one rich in raw, nutrient-dense foods. The good news is that there are some convenient options for consumers. As society is slowly realizing that diseases are on the rise—and Americans have many more health ailments than ever before—we are starting to look at the causes and the variables around us. Because of this awakening, most of the large chain grocery stores now house a decent-sized organic and natural foods section. This is where you can trust that the ingredients are pure, and you can find specialty items, like dairy-free or gluten-free choices.

Another option is to find a local farm and commit to a farm share. This means that once a week (or every other, because you can set the frequency) you pick up locally grown, in-season, organic fruits and vegetables. If you want to take the next step and start shopping for all healthy-living products, cleaning essentials, beauty products, and organic foods, there are stores that specialize in that too. There are a ton of what I call "one-stop health shops."

The bottom line is, as a society, we are slowly making the correlation between our crazy hectic lifestyles (and the need for fast food) and the astronomical levels of stress that we are all dealing with these days. This face-paced, go-go-go lifestyle is affecting our health, our family bonds, and our overall happiness and well-being.

This chapter is not meant to sway you into completely overhauling your diet like I did, but to plant a seed in your mind so you slowly start to make more informed purchasing decisions. I also hope you will start to research all I've mentioned here (to the level that you're comfortable) so you can begin to want nothing but the best for yourself—food and lifestyle included.

Now let's talk exercise. Did you know exercise can boost your happiness levels? Well, it can! Without getting too scientific, working out increases the release of endorphins from your brain to your body. This process makes you happier, more alert, and sharper. It boosts memory and helps you sleep more soundly.

I can go on and on about WHY exercise is so important, yet for some reason, some of us still view it as a punishment. We've been programmed to believe eating balanced and clean leads to feelings of deprivation. (Hence, the reason I despise the word "diet.") Maybe you have it in your head that exercise is only for gym goers who "like that kinda thing" (and you only do it if you want to lose weight). However, I encourage you to treat your body properly, because you love it—NOT because you hate it and judge it.

We can all use a little movement in our lives. It will help reduce stress and can be a great outlet. My family is known to literally drop everything, blast the music, and dance around the kitchen. And guess what? That's exercise! You don't have to be hammering out crazy workout programs; find what you love and DO THAT! It's that simple.

This healthy lifestyle can also help you socially. Find a community of people who make happiness and health a priority. Learn from them and ask questions. Join an online support group (there are tons). I used to run some groups myself, so why not start your own? It's a place where you can have your spirits lifted and get encouragement along your new journey of awakening and bettering yourself as you tackle whatever adversity you encounter. Being surrounded by people who think positively and do right by their bodies will surely inspire you (even if you don't realize it right away).

Lastly, Google everything. There are tons of clean eating and healthy recipes that replicate some of your favorite snacks and meals. Remember, it's not about deprivation, it's a gift to do the best you can possibly do for your body—your temple.

Lesson learned! You are what you eat and, YES, exercise is important! You make time for what is important to you. If you want to feel good physically, you CAN! Are you willing to do what you need to do to get there, or are you continuing to make excuses as to why you can't?

Ask yourself: On a typical day, what does your food intake look like? Are you open to changing some of your eating habits so you can feel better? If yes, what can you do to get started?

Message for the Soul: You can't control everything, but you can control what you do with your body.

● ● ● ● ●

Chapter 10

All That and a Bag of Chips

Have you ever heard that expression, "She's all that and a bag of chips!"? It implies someone has confidence and everything going for her. When I hear that phrase, I visualize a striking woman entering a room (imagine spotlight, smoke machine, and fan for the dramatic hair-blowing visual here). Her presence is so powerful she makes heads turn. She has a fierceness about her that can't be broken. She makes people crave her company just because she is who she is. Her energy is positive and her "way" is just attractive, sexy, vibrant, and full of life!

Doesn't *"she"* sound amazing?

These days, everything seems to be about the hustle and bustle. You're programmed to be on autopilot, and your time is so limited. Many things fall to the wayside, or they're put on the back burner so "life" can be tended to. This depletes your spirit. So what makes *her* (the all-that-and-a-bag-of-chips woman) so different?

Why is *she* so put-together while you feel like you're just barely keeping your head above water? (And most of the time, you actually feel more like a sinking ship?) It's actually quite simple: *She* has learned her self-worth. *She* takes the time to love and nurture herself. *She* fills her own cup and then has an overflow for others. You've been programmed to think you need to put others first. In reality, your own needs are just as important—if not more important!

It's not selfish; it's the key to true happiness.

During my second bout with cancer, I've seen the difference in the "before and after." Before my diagnosis, I believed my sole purpose in life was to help others. I determined my self-worth by people's opinions of me and the encounters I had with them. I've discovered when you put your own happiness in the hands of others, it does NOT end well.

Why? Because we all come from different walks of life and experiences. We're very good at projecting our fears and unresolved issues onto each other. So if you are internalizing people's behavior and using that to fuel yourself, you run the risk of running on an empty tank (and one day, the car just stops running!).

I learned a pivotal lesson just recently. It took a lifetime of turmoil and chaos for me to actually realize that I MATTER. The people around me were used to me being there. I was *that* person who was everyone's biggest cheerleader. Some nights, I'd literally be ripped out of my sleep, because I remembered someone had a job interview and I *needed* to wish her good luck, or I'd remember a friend was taking a trip and I *needed* to wish him safe travels.

Looking back, it sounds silly. I think my need for others to "not feel alone" and "know they are cared about" came from me looking at myself in the mirror. In reality, I needed those things. My internal drive to make people happy completely took over my life. I guess part of me never felt good enough unless I was positively affecting those around me. That's a big burden to bear, isn't it?

Unfortunately, no one ever told me people come with their own set of expectations and blueprints based on how their lives started. I never got a heads-up that relationships built on *need* usually don't end very well. I didn't realize the impact it had made on the stress in my life until I got diagnosed the second time.

When I found out I had breast cancer, many people in my life came together. But many others scattered. I'd been there for so many others—yet when I was down-and-out, I felt completely alone. People didn't know how to deal with me not being as accessible to them because I had the overbearing new role of fighting for my life, again.

After all the dust settles with a trauma or tragedy, people on the periphery go on with their lives, but you're faced with an adversity you just can't escape. I learned the difference between friendship and codependency. I learned relationships that are unconditional should be easy, not hard work.

There are plenty of stressors in a day, so the people you choose to have in your circle should enhance your life—not cloud it. You need your tribe to be "all that and a bag of chips." The people in your boat need to be rowing alongside you, not drilling holes in it.

Unfortunately for me, I was faced with the reality that there was a lot of toxicity in my life. When you face something big, it forces you to re-evaluate your life and who is in it. It was like I had finally woken up to smell those coffee beans, and the universe was screaming out to me:

MAKE SOME CHANGES!
LOVE YOURSELF!
YOU ARE ENOUGH!

Being enlightened is like a bright light bulb that goes off in your head. Once your conscious mind is aware of what needs to happen to move away from situations or relationships that no longer serve you, it seems doors begin to open everywhere—doors that lead to opportunities, doors that introduce you to the next group of people who will ultimately help you learn the next set of life's lessons, and doors that, if you allow them to, give you direct access to all the tools you need to be that girl (or guy) who is *all that and a bag of chips.*

Go ahead and be that fierce being everyone else wants to be around.

Be the confident bright light you're ultimately meant to be in this world.

Be the new, more grown-up YOU who understands the importance of putting yourself first so you can be the best version of you.

Be the go-getter who believes in yourself.

Be the one who eliminates toxic people from your life (and your heart.) Surround yourself with eagles who want to fly!

Lesson learned! Put yourself first. Love yourself enough to fuel yourself daily. You have the right to choose bright energy around you. You don't need to be stuck in unhealthy relationships or situations. If need be, set boundaries or walk away. It's not your job to fill other people's cups by absorbing the brunt of their insecurities and inner turmoil. As Dr. Seuss says, "Be who you are and say how you feel, because those who mind don't matter and those who matter don't mind!"

Ask yourself: Are you the kind of person who sets yourself on fire just to keep others warm?

Message for the soul: "If you want to fly, get rid of everything that weighs you down!"

—Unknown

• • • • •

Chapter 11

Gratitude Changes Your Attitude

Have you ever woken up on the wrong side of the bed? Maybe you had a bad dream. (I'm notorious for having a nightmare and waking up feeling as if it were true.)

When you have a lot on your mind, it can be easy to allow your mind to wander down dark paths. Days like that can feel like nothing will make you feel better.

You are just in a rotten mood, and tomorrow will be better.

It doesn't have to be that way. I want you to view your life a single day at a time. Tomorrow hasn't happened yet, so there's no sense worrying about it. And yesterday—well, you don't drive your car backward, now do you?

The present moment is a gift. It's the only time you'll ever experience this NOW, so why would you ever settle for anything other than great?

Truth be told, some circumstances don't lend themselves toward greatness, but you can make yourself feel better despite what's happening around you. If you are dealing with a death or trauma, you might be asking yourself, "What good could I actually feel right now?" The answer is plenty!

Gratitude will not change what has happened in your life. It won't erase hard times, but it will help guide your mindset to a more positive path. This way you can make the most of today, regardless of any undesirable situations.

Think about it. You wake up every morning with the chance to have a clean slate—a fresh start to embrace the day any way you choose. And, yes, it's under your control.

Take me for example: I was diagnosed with two different types of cancer in two years—diagnosed the night before my fortieth birthday (which I was so looking forward to).

Most people would say I have every reason to be angry and depressed and play the victim. Instead, I choose to thrive. After all, I don't know how long I'll be blessed to be on this earth, so I'll be damned if I waste any of my time feeling badly.

Every morning—and I mean every single morning—as soon as my eyes open, I practice gratitude.

I start by naming three things I'm whole-heartedly grateful for. It almost always has to do with my husband and my children. Within seconds, I feel surrounded by love; pure, white light; and the unconditional presence of

God. My mind has been put on the track of optimism, and I can see that no matter how low life can get, there is always something to be grateful for.

It's a routine that can take five seconds, yet its power to protect your day can be used as often as you need it. While driving to work, I often find I'll notice a particularly beautiful sky and thank God for it. I look around at the home my husband and I worked so hard to put together; I notice how it depicts every single little piece of who we are—that warms my heart and makes me want to give thanks.

Throughout the day, I will sometimes be grateful if I notice someone smile or hold a door open for me. Your thanks can be as simple or as grand as you want it to be. The key is to be aware of how very much there is in your life that you can feel blessed about.

If you choose to be grateful, I promise you, you will change your life. It will begin to slowly teach you how amazing it feels to have the power to see the good.

The miracle of thankfulness is that it shifts your perception so much that it can change the way you see the world.

My challenge to you is this: Tomorrow, the moment your eyes open, take a deep cleansing breath in. As you breathe in, complete this phrase to the universe THREE TIMES:

(Inhale slowly.) Thank you for …

(Exhale slowly, emptying all of the air in your lungs as you push out thoughts of negative people and situations that cloud your mind.)

(Inhale slowly.) Thank you for …

(Exhale slowly, emptying your self doubt.)

(Inhale slowly.) Thank you for …

(Exhale slowly, emptying any final lingering darkness left in your heart.)

If you add this into your daily morning routine, you'll be sure to feel an instant sense of peace as you begin your day.

As this practice becomes more natural, you can begin to sprinkle gratefulness into other parts of your day.

I love sending people quick texts or voice messages letting them know how lucky I feel to have them in my life. Think about it … now not only are you feeling better, but you are spreading your happiness and appreciation into the lives of others around you. It's like a snowball effect that will begin to shift your higher frequency. In turn, you attract much better things.

This may seem like a simple task, but it's one of the most powerful things you can do to increase positivity in your life. It opens the door to power and wisdom and allows you to see that you can truly extract happiness from common, everyday things.

There is so much to be thankful for—just look around!

Lesson learned! There is ALWAYS something to be thankful for.

Ask yourself: Are you willing to decide that no matter what comes your way, you will find a grateful heart?

Message for the soul: "When I'm worried and cannot sleep, I count my blessings instead of sheep."

— Bing Crosby

• • • • •

Chapter 12

Being Versus Doing

As you're approaching the end of this book, I hope your wheels are turning. My wish for everyone who reads this book is that you feel like it has been (and will continue to be) a companion during some rough times. The universe has shaken you enough to awaken you; where are you going to go from here? I hope by now you've shifted from feeling lost and hopeless to having a little more clarity and focus.

I have never been the type of person who blended into a crowd. It always seemed to me that something dramatic and big was happening in my life. Most of my forty years have been spent feeling confused and misunderstood. Now, though, I realize it was all a part of the master plan—and it feels so good to be lost in the right direction!

Now is the time to make a pledge—one you must fulfill for yourself. Promise that you will reject the status quo and start taking drastic measures to get your life back on track. You are an asset to this world, and everyone is waiting for you to unlock your potential (whatever that may be). We are all given one life to live. Are you going to let circumstances steer you in the direction of success (whatever success means to you), or will you let it take you down?

There are no limitations on our lives, aside from the ones we put on ourselves. My hope is that you begin to believe in yourself and all the greatness locked within you. I pray your life is filled with adventure and you rise above whatever adversity made you pick up this book. Change is sometimes needed to better yourself, and it's a lifelong endeavor.

You live and you learn. Rinse and repeat!

You can always be a little better, stand a little taller, love a little deeper.

You can pick a different path and walk a different walk.

You can find forgiveness, joy, and pure happiness in every day!

You CAN change your life; it takes one single step, and that step is your decision to try (silent round of applause because you picked up this book to help kick-start your journey!).

I'm a firm believer in sending positive mantras to the brain, so I want to leave you with this:

You are not perfect (none of us are), BUT you are enough!

You are not where you want to be in your life, BUT you are where you are supposed to be right now!

You are not doing it all, BUT you are doing something, and that is a step in the right direction!

And I'd love to leave you with my favorite mantra that I personally need to remind myself of daily: YOU ARE ENOUGH!

Do NOT get stuck in the rut of just "being" and existing. You are meant to thrive, so use this book as a springboard to feel empowered and start "doing!"

Now go out there and rock this amazing life of yours, my new friend!

I believe in you!

●　●　●　●　●

Dedication

This book is dedicated to the people who didn't scatter, the ones who held my heart and protected it unconditionally, and the ones who believed I would turn my trial into a triumph!

A special thank you to my AM for believing I could spread my wings and for showing me I'm capable of anything. Thank you for believing in me!

To my husband,

You and I have moved mountains together. You have been my rock through it all and I promise to always drive us forward, together!

Lastly, To my beautiful children,

May you always know your worth. May you believe in yourself as fiercely as I believe in you! I will always be your biggest fan!

We did it!

#bucketlist #riseup #withoneblink

Made in the USA
Coppell, TX
19 November 2020

41628248R00049